Foreign Investment in the United States:

What Does It Signal

A Committee for Economic Development
Program Statement on National Policy

CED

Library of Congress Cataloging-in-Publication Data

Foreign Investment in the United States : What Does it Signal? : a statement by
the Program Committee of the Committee for Economic Development.
p. cm.
"September 1990."
Includes bibliographical references.
ISBN 0-87186-116-X (paperback) : $10.00
1 Investments, Foreign—United States.
I. Committee on Economic Development.
Program Committee.
HG4910.F647 1990
332.6'73'0973—dc20   90-15021
                          CIP

Printed in the United States
Design: Rowe & Ballantine

Committee For Economic Development

477 Madison Avenue
New York, New York 10022
(212) 688-2063

1700 K Street, NW
Washington, DC 20006
(202) 296-5860

Foreign Investment in the United States: What Does It Signal?

A Statement by the Program Committee of the
Committee for Economic Development

Table of Contents

Responsibility for CED Program Statements

The publication of this statement is authorized by the regulations of the Research and Policy Committee that empower the Program Committee to issue statements within the framework of policies previously stated by the Research and Policy Committee.

Proposals in this statement are derived from principles expressed in a series of policy statements that deal with international economics and international trade and investment, including: *Transnational Corporations and Developing Countries* (1981), *Toll of the Twin Deficits* (1987), *Finance and Third World Economic Growth* (1988), *New Dynamics in the Global Economy* (1988), *Strengthening U.S.-Japan Economic Relations* (1989), *Who Should Be Liable? A Guide To Policy for Dealing With Risk* (1989), and *Breaking New Ground in U.S. Trade Policy* (1990).

Purpose of This Statement

The rise in foreign investment in this country has prompted much heated debate on whether such investment is, as one end of the argument goes, an economic boon to this nation or, at the other end of the debate spectrum, a threat to our national security.

Much of this debate has, unfortunately, been conducted on political and often emotional grounds, without enough regard for the relevant facts. Our intention in this statement has been to examine the extent of foreign investment in the United States and to let our conclusions be guided by the economic facts and by the actual effects that foreign investment is having and can have on the U.S. economy and society.

In this statement we pose some of what we feel are the best questions to ask about foreign investment in the United States, and we attempt to answer them in a brief, balanced, and forthright format.

A HISTORY OF INTERNATIONAL LEADERSHIP

For nearly fifty years, the effects of the international economy on our own have been a key interest of CED trustees, as have been ways to encourage healthy international economic growth.

Our earliest statements supported the Marshall Plan and the Bretton Woods agreement, and they were followed in the 1950s, 1960s, and 1970s with reports dealing with the most critical international economic issues of those years.

In the past decade, the U.S. trade imbalance with other nations has grown, and CED has focused on what steps our nation and those abroad need to take to restore a healthier trade balance and a sounder domestic economic footing.

Our 1987 policy statement, *Toll of the Twin Deficits* made clear the broad connections between our big budget deficits, our low saving rate, and our big trade deficit. Our most recent statement, *Breaking New Ground in U.S. Trade Policy* (1990) called for a broad-based set of strategies to open foreign markets while at the same time guarding U.S. business interests from unfair trade practices.

ACKNOWLEDGMENTS

I would like to thank the expanded CED Program Committee (whose members are listed on page iv) for the knowledge and experience they contributed to this statement. Special thanks are due to Robert C. Holland, director of this project, for his clarity and expertise in crafting this document. Dr. Holland, who recently retired as president of CED after 14 years of service, is now the organization's Senior Economic Consultant.

Finally, we are deeply grateful to The Chase Manhattan Bank whose generous support has made possible broad distribution of this report. Additional funding for dissemination of this publication was provided by Citibank.

Dean P. Phypers
Chairman, CED Program Committee

Summary

Foreign capital funds have been pouring into the United States in the largest volumes ever experienced by this generation of Americans. Much more capital has been coming in than going out, in association with the big U.S. trade deficits. These huge inflows are raising all sorts of questions in many quarters in this country.

Are these striking net capital inflows from abroad good or bad for us? In a word, both. These foreign investments help boost our current standard of living. But they also pose problems, although not for the reasons that grab big headlines.

The most serious and growing problem stemming from this surge of net foreign investment in the United States is the big future net debt-service burden due foreigners that we are in process of creating. A major force attracting those foreign investments is the pulling power of the penchant for high consumption and low saving that Americans have developed in recent decades. Basically, therefore, the surge of net foreign investment into the United States is a signal that we ought to reconsider our "spend now, save later" attitude.

To explore this phenomenal rise in foreign investment more systematically, this program statement poses eleven questions that we believe are the most useful to ask about foreign investment and provides answers to them. Those questions and short answers appear in this summary. Fuller answers are presented in the text that follows.

QUESTION	ANSWER
1. What do we mean by foreign investment in the United States?	It takes two forms: *direct* investment, involving the foreign ownership and control of American businesses and properties, and *portfolio* investment, involving the ownership of other private and government securities and bank deposits.
2. How big is foreign investment in the United States?	Foreign *portfolio* investment in the United States is estimated to have a current value of nearly $1.7 trillion, about one and three-quarters times the size of U.S. portfolio investments abroad. The current value of *direct* investment is harder to gauge, but a rough estimate is that foreign *direct* investment in the United States is worth about $0.5 trillion. The total of U.S. direct investments abroad is about one and a half times larger. But foreign holdings are growing faster than U.S. holdings in both categories.
3. Which countries are the biggest direct investors in the United States?	The United Kingdom is by far the largest *direct* investor in the United States, followed by Japan and the Netherlands. Of these, however, the British and Japanese holdings are growing the fastest.

4. Why does foreign investment come into the United States?

There are three main reasons. First, it is attracted by relatively high rates of return available in this country, which in turn are related to our high consumption and relatively low national saving ratio. Second, the United States is a politically safe place to invest. Third, an attraction important for *direct* investment is that some foreign producers like to buy or build plants in the United States to be close to their customers in the big U.S. market and inside any U.S. trade barriers that might apply.

5. What good does foreign investment do for the United States?

It is a source of capital and foreign exchange. In addition, *direct* foreign investments can bring benefits in the form of new productive capacity, technology, know-how, and jobs.

6. What are the biggest potential drawbacks of such heavy net foreign investment flows into the United States?

They come not from *direct* investment but from the fast-rising level of foreign *portfolio* investment. If it soars further upward in future years, it portends a growing net foreign debt-service burden and eventual mounting risks of financial instability.

7. Is there a threat to U.S. national security from foreign ownership of key U.S. manufacturing plants?

To the extent that there is a potential threat, this country is equipped to guard against it. The President can bar any foreign investments that pose such a threat, and the Defense Department should be able to put safeguard conditions into its defense contracts with such firms.

8. How can we be sure foreign-owned companies in the United States will behave responsibly?

By and large, they are subject to the same regulations and pressures to behave responsibly as U.S.-owned firms are. Any action or conduct contrary to U.S. law or regulations should be punished with an appropriate penalty.

9. Is foreign ownership of U.S. real estate bad?

No. It may wound our pride, but it presents no economic threat.

10. These answers make it sound like the pluses add up to more than the minuses. Can that be so?

Yes. Well-placed foreign investments and their trade-related benefits are not a zero-sum game. There is a positive net gain that all can share when such transactions are voluntarily and constructively entered into by both sides. But if allowed to continue, trade and investment imbalances as big as those the United States is now incurring will detract from our future gains.

11. Do we need more international rules regarding foreign direct investment?

Yes. We need to negotiate a comprehensive international agreement covering investment across national borders. The General Agreement on Tariffs and Trade (GATT) negotiations on trade-related investment measures (TRIMs) now proceeding in Geneva are a step forward. Worthwhile results in these negotiations could help to make the shared benefits of foreign trade and investment even greater.

1. What Do We Mean by Foreign Investment in the United States?

Foreign investment flows can be divided into two types: *direct* investment and *portfolio* investment.

Foreign *direct* investment is defined as the foreign ownership and control of real estate or commercial facilities in the United States. The various forms by which a foreign parent company makes direct investments in a U.S. affiliate include the provision of equity capital, reinvested earnings, and net lending by the parent to the affiliate.

Foreign *portfolio* (or indirect) investment includes the foreign ownership of all other U.S. financial assets (i.e., those that do not convey ownership or control of a U.S. firm). These include federal, state, and local government securities; corporate stocks; municipal bonds; and bank deposits. For the most part, assets purchased for portfolio investment are easily sold, moved, or cashed.

The word *foreign* in *foreign investment* also needs defining. The legal definition that the Commerce Department uses for its statistical tabulations is: "Foreign in a geographic sense means that which is situated outside the United States, or which belongs to, or is characteristic of a country other than the United States."[1] In practical terms, this definition is interpreted as basing the nationality of a firm on the location of its parent company's headquarters.

Given the increasing globalization of business operations, however, this definition is not an adequate description of what is actually taking place. Increasingly, multinational corporations are producing, employing, buying, selling, and servicing in a number of different countries. In some cases, firms that originated in one country now do most of their production and sales elsewhere.

Despite these confusing aspects, we still need a practical working definition of *foreign*, even if it is limited or imperfect. Therefore, for the purposes of this statement, we will use the U.S. Commerce Department's definition.

2. How Big Is Foreign Investment in the United States?

It is helpful to approach this question by first recalling the several different ways in which foreign investment in the United States can grow: through the foreign acquisition of more liquid or marketable U.S. financial assets; through the construction of new,

---

[1]Code of Federal Regulations, Title 15, part 806.7B.

FIGURE 1

Foreign Investment Positions

Trillions of Dollars in Current Value

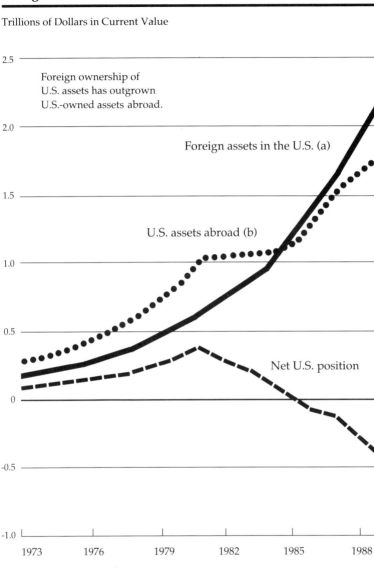

a: Includes foreign official assets in the United States.
b: Excludes U.S. official reserve assets.

SOURCE: U.S. Department of Commerce, Bureau of Economic Analysis; for estimated current values of foreign direct investments, Lois Stekler and Guy Stevens, "The Adequacy of U.S. Direct Investment Data."

"greenfield" (i.e., built from scratch) production facilities within the United States by foreign companies; through the foreign purchase of U.S. real estate; and through the acquisition of a controlling share in an existing U.S. firm.

Once a foreign firm has acquired U.S. assets in one of these ways, the value of those assets can subsequently change in one or all of three ways: by retaining subsequent operating earnings (or losses), by capital appreciation (or depreciation), and by changes in the value of the foreign firm's currency compared with that of the U.S. dollar. (This last change does not affect any of the numbers in this statement because they are all stated in U.S. dollars, but it is a factor that foreign firms have to take into account for many purposes.)

The most comprehensive measure of the size of foreign investment in the United States is the current value of all the U.S. assets owned by foreign investors. A rough estimate is about $2.2 trillion. Figure 1 on page 7 shows the U.S. net international investment position through successive years. (It should be noted that most of the components of this aggregate figure are estimated, and some of those estimates are more conjectural than others.)

The largest share of this total foreign investment in the United States consists of *portfolio* investments. These holdings totaled nearly $1.7 trillion at current value at the end of 1989. Although this figure is large, it amounts to only a small fraction of the U.S. total of securities and bank deposits outstanding. By comparison, such U.S. portfolio investment holdings by foreigners are roughly one and three-quarters times as large in total as the portfolio investment abroad by U.S. citizens, organizations, and governments (see Figure 2, page 9). That margin has been widening rapidly in recent years because of the upsurge in such foreign investment.

This portfolio-inflow measure incorporates most of the foreign-owned assets that can be sold quickly and on which future payments of foreign debt service need to be made. Therefore, it casts the clearest light on the problems of foreign debt-service burdens and potential financial instability associated with increasing foreign investment in the United States. (See question 6 for more details.)

The second major category, foreign *direct* investment in the United States, is more difficult to estimate. The official government statistics, published by the Department of Commerce, estimate direct investments at book value (which in most cases is roughly equal to the original cost of acquisition). Based solely on these book values, 1989 estimates show foreign direct investment in the United States at $401 billion and U.S. direct investment abroad at $373 billion.

FIGURE 2

Foreign Portfolio Investment Positions

Trillions of Dollars in Current Value

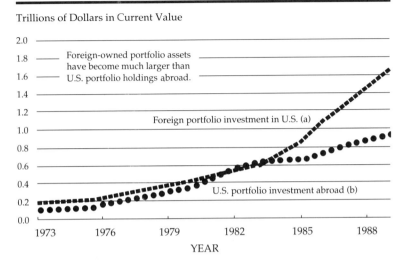

YEAR

FIGURE 3

Foreign Direct Investment Positions

Trillions of Dollars in Current Value

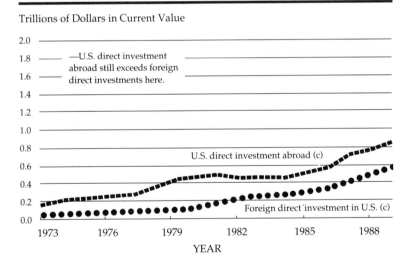

YEAR

a: Includes foreign official assets in the United States.

b: Excludes U.S. official reserve assets.

c: For standard statistical purposes, direct investment is defined by the Commerce Department to mean the ownership or control of 10 percent or more of the voting rights of a U.S. firm.

SOURCE: U.S. Department of Commerce, Bureau of Economic Analysis; for estimated current values of foreign direct investments, Lois Stekler and Guy Stevens, "The Adequacy of U.S. Direct Investment Data."

However, because such book values do not take into account postpurchase changes in value, they do not tell the entire story. When current values of such direct investments are approximated by adjustments to take into account inflation and exchange rate changes, U.S. direct investments abroad are worth about one and a half times as much as foreign direct investment here (in 1989, roughly $800 billion compared with $500 billion). (See Figure 3, page 9.)

Although U.S. direct investments abroad at current value are still worth significantly more than foreign direct investments here, the latter have been rising more rapidly than the former in the past three years. However, these foreign holdings, like foreign portfolio investments, still constitute only a small fraction of the total value of American land, factories, and other buildings.

*　*　*

Of all the magnitudes mentioned here, the hardest to estimate are postpurchase changes in the value of direct investments overseas. The estimates we used here were developed by economists Lois Stekler and Guy Stevens, based on subsequent changes in national inflation rates and exchange rates. Figures 4 and 5 on page 11 present data for foreign direct investments with and without this component included and thereby indicate the increasing importance over time of such appreciation in the dollar value of U.S.-owned assets abroad.

3. Which Countries Are the Biggest Direct Investors in the United States?

This question has to be answered in terms of the net *book* value of foreign direct investments rather than *current* value. We have no good estimates of the latter by country of ownership. (See question 2 for more details.)

The United Kingdom is far and away the largest foreign direct investor in the United States. It accounts for more than a quarter of the total and holds roughly twice as much as the second- and third-ranking countries, Japan and the Netherlands (see Figure 6, page 12). No other single country holds as much as one-tenth of the total of foreign direct investment in the United States.

In the more than doubling of foreign direct investment holdings in book value terms that has taken place since 1985, Britain and Japan have led the way; each has about tripled its holdings. The Netherlands has shown growth in holdings in more moderate

FIGURE 4

U.S. Direct Investment Abroad, Comparison of Current and Book Values

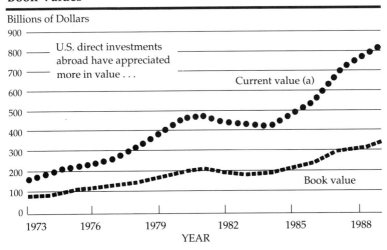

Billions of Dollars

U.S. direct investments abroad have appreciated more in value . . .

Current value (a)

Book value

FIGURE 5

Foreign Direct Investment in the United States, Comparison of Current and Book Values, 1973 to 1989

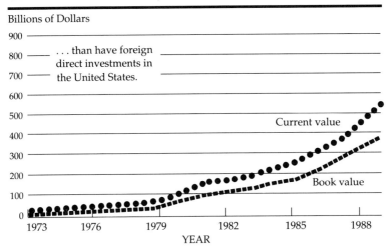

Billions of Dollars

. . . than have foreign direct investments in the United States.

Current value

Book value

a: Over the years, U.S. direct investments overseas have appreciated substantially more in estimated current value than have foreign direct investments in the United States. This phenomenon is believed to be partly due to the fact that the bulk of U.S. overseas direct investments have been owned longer and therefore have had more time to appreciate.

SOURCE: U.S. Department of Commerce, Bureau of Economic Analysis; for estimated current values of foreign direct investments, Lois Stekler and Guy Stevens, "The Adequacy of U.S. Direct Investment Data."

dimensions through most of the 1980s. However, since a good share of these Dutch holdings go back a number of years and even decades, a relatively greater increase in postpurchase value (not measured in these statistics) is probably embedded in them. If current value were the test, such postpurchase increases might be enough to keep the Netherlands still ranked above Japan in 1989 as a direct investor in the United States.

It is worth remembering that relatively few if any of these direct investments are owned by the *governments* of Britain, Japan, and the Netherlands. They are owned instead by individuals, partnerships, and corporations headquartered in these countries.

FIGURE 6

Foreign Direct Investment in the United States by Selected Foreign Nations

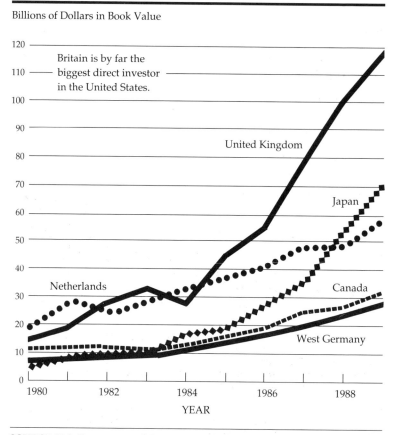

Billions of Dollars in Book Value

SOURCE: U.S. Department of Commerce, Bureau of Economic Analysis.

4. Why Does Foreign Investment Come into the United States?

Given the size and complexity of the U.S. economy, there are many reasons why foreign savers and owners of capital funds might wish to invest at least some of those funds here. However, three reasons seem to stand out.

First, foreigners are drawn to invest money in the United States because it is judged a relatively safe place to keep such funds. In general, property rights are well respected in this country. The United States is militarily strong, and its political and legal structures are comparatively stable. Certain other locations, such as Switzerland, also have at least some of these advantages, but the United States can absorb more investable foreign funds. Generally, these safety considerations weigh more heavily in the thinking of foreigners interested in making *portfolio* investment than those seeking *direct* investment.

Second, foreign producers are attracted to make *direct* investments in plants in the United States because of the net advantage of having some of their productive facilities close to their current and hoped-for customers in the big American marketplace. This reason has become increasingly important in recent years. Foreign manufacturers of certain products are finding it can be a distinct competitive advantage to have U.S. plants capable of making speedy deliveries to customers. Such close contact can also help them to stay more attuned to changing U.S. customer needs and desires. A further benefit of such proximity can loom large when trade frictions produce, or threaten to produce, barriers to the free import of goods from the producer's home country.

Third, the U.S. economy is generating demands for credit and equity funds from businesses, consumers, and governments that total well in excess of the amounts available from domestic saving. To make up the difference, we are relying on funds from foreign investors. We attract such foreign funds primarily by offering *relatively* high *real* rates of return on earning assets foreigners can buy. Wise foreign investors compare the expected rates of return they can earn here with what they can earn at home or in other attractive countries, with due allowance for prospective differences in the rates of inflation and risks of principal loss in those markets and in currency exchange rates. Although U.S. real rates of interest on investments went up and down in the 1980s, on average they were relatively high, particularly when compared with rates in the Japanese and German markets, where the biggest proportions of investable saving have been accruing.

Even while these factors were attracting foreign investment to the United States, American investors were finding some investment opportunities in foreign countries that suited their purposes very well. Thus, the gross total of U.S. investment overseas continued to mount even as the gross volume of foreign investment in the United States surged upward. The latter was growing more than twice as fast as the former after 1982, however; and as a consequence, the net international investment position of the United States turned negative before the end of the 1980s.

The recent substantial increases in net foreign portfolio investment in the United States can be attributed to a large extent to the combination of our low private saving rate and our big federal budget deficits (which amount to government *dissaving*). The U.S. rate of net national saving has for years averaged well below that in other industrialized countries (see Figure 7, page 15).

Moreover, the United States invests a higher proportion of its private saving in residential construction than most other countries do, and new homes do not add directly to U.S. productive capacity. To be sure, U.S. citizens have improved their financial status by having the real value of their homes and other existing assets increase more than the real value of their liabilities, and some experts like to regard such an improvement as additional saving or wealth. However, none of this kind of gain in wealth frees real resources for productive investment the way saving rather than spending of income does. The upshot is that in the amount of private saving available for productive investment, the United States ranks relatively low among major countries.

As for *government dissaving*, federal deficits have been at record peacetime levels during the 1980s. The resulting adverse economic effects have been substantial. First, the huge increases in U.S. Treasury borrowing combined with the low rate of private saving have held up real U.S. interest rate costs and thereby constrained the growth of domestic capital investment. Second, the relatively high domestic interest rates have helped to attract foreign capital and have consequently held up the value of the dollar. This has left U.S. producers less competitive and increased our trade deficits. Third, there has been explosive growth in federal interest payments, an increasing share of which is going abroad. If this continues, U.S. interest and dividend payments to foreigners will grow progressively larger than U.S. earnings on foreign investment (see Figure 8, page 16). In order to cover that emerging gap (what the experts call the *net foreign debt-service burden*), the United States will be impelled in the future to consume and invest less than it produces and borrows. This will take a larger bite out of our future standard of living.

The globalization of financial markets has both positive and negative implications for the U.S. foreign debt-service burden. As financial markets become more global, it becomes easier for capital to move from country to country, and the owners of capital become more willing to have a sizable share of their funds invested in other countries when the rates of return there look better. In turn, this works to reduce the relative margin of return that a sound borrower has to offer to attract a foreign investor.

On the other hand, the globalization of financial markets also makes it easier for owners of investable funds to respond to attractive new investment opportunities outside the United States. A current case in point is the opening of Eastern Europe, which is

FIGURE 7

Net National Saving, 1960 to 1988 (Annual Averages)

Percent of GDP

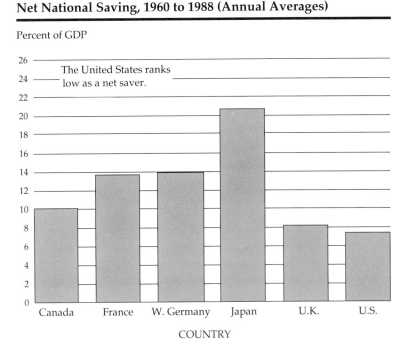

COUNTRY

Note 1: Gross domestic product (GDP), measures the output produced by factors in the United States and, unlike gross national product (GNP), excludes net earnings from the rest of the world.

Note 2: Net national saving is defined as the difference between current receipts and current disbursements of each nation's individuals, businesses, and governments. It is derived by deducting government and private final consumption from national disposable income.

SOURCE: Organization for Economic Cooperation and Development (OECD), *National Accounts, Main Aggregates*, Volume I, 1960-88 (Paris, France, 1990).

16

attracting much attention from firms headquartered in Western Europe, the United States, and Japan. If Eastern Europe attracts large amounts of direct investment from such firms or even large amounts of aid from those governments that is not matched by offsetting budget cuts or higher taxes, U.S. borrowers will have to pay higher real rates of return than otherwise would be needed in order to keep attracting the financing they seek.

Because the large net foreign capital inflows during the 1980s have relieved the crowding-out phenomenon of large U.S. govern-

FIGURE 8

Foreign Debt Service, 1960 to 1989

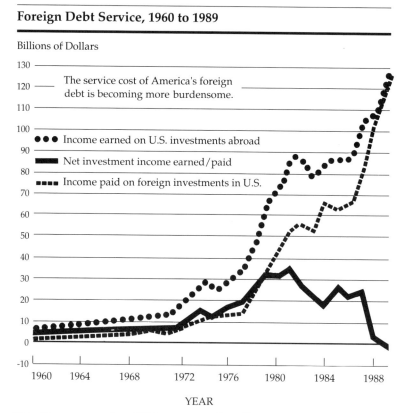

Note: "Income earned on U.S. investments abroad" consists of receipts from U.S. direct investments in foreign assets, other private receipts, and U.S. government receipts. Similarly, "income paid on foreign investments in U.S." consists of payments to foreigners from foreign-owned direct investment in the United States, other private payments, and U.S. government payments (which includes interest payments on the national debt to foreigners). "Net investment income earned/paid" is the difference between income earned and income paid.

SOURCE: U.S. Department of Commerce, Bureau of Economic Analysis.

ment borrowing, they have permitted us to sustain our investment outlays for plants and equipment; without those, the U.S. economy would be lagging even farther behind. But they have only *permitted* it; they have not *compelled* it. In practice, we are using an imprudently large share of such inflows to increase our consumption rather than our productive investment.

To correct that situation, we need to concentrate on reducing the federal deficit and curtailing our private-sector proclivity to spend now and save later. National saving in both the public and the private sectors needs to increase significantly. Only then will U.S. productivity and competitiveness improve vigorously, and only then will the potential risks associated with increasing foreign investment be reduced. (These risks are discussed at length in the answer to question 6.)*

5. What Good Does Foreign Investment Do for the United States?

In recent years, particularly in the press and the government, much of the discussion about increasing foreign investment in the United States has focused on the associated costs and risks, while the large potential benefits have been mostly overlooked in the national headlines. But as we suggested in the answer to question 4, foreign investment has many positive effects on the U.S. economy. In general, those fall into three categories: provision of needed capital and foreign exchange, trade-related investment benefits, and broader socioeconomic benefits.

PROVISION OF NEEDED CAPITAL AND FOREIGN EXCHANGE

Foreign capital inflows have to an important extent financed our recent substantial excesses in government and private expenditure beyond what we have produced domestically. It is the counterpart of our excess of imports over exports, and those extra imports have enabled us to raise our current consumption while limiting the rise in prices and interest rates that would have been necessary in the absence of foreign investment inflows. In other words, in the absence of this net inward flow of capital, we could not incur our enormous trade and current-account deficits and therefore could not indulge our propensity for high consumption and low saving.

If in the current circumstances the inflow of foreign investment is sharply reduced or reversed (either by foreign investors chang-

---

* See memorandum by JAMES Q. RIORDAN (page 32).

ing their minds or by the United States enacting restrictions), the consequences would be painful. We would not be receiving enough foreign exchange to sustain our current level of spending on foreign goods and services. U.S. prices and interest rates (nominal and real) would be driven upward, and interest-sensitive consumer expenditures (e.g., for homes and automobiles) would thereby decline. Moreover, as a result of increased interest rates, domestic investment by U.S. businesses would also suffer, falling to even lower levels at a time when our economy would need it to be increased for competitiveness reasons. Although our international accounts would be forced into balance, the standard of living that Americans currently enjoy would be curtailed sharply as both consumption and private investment were reduced.

Yet, the benefits of the unfettered movement of capital across national borders are not limited merely to transferring funds from excess-saver nations to an excessive spender such as the United States. Even if the net balance of international capital flows to and from the United States were zero, substantial benefits would still result from the continuing increases that can be expected in the gross total of cross-border financial transactions. These transactions permit a more efficient allocation of world resources than would otherwise occur, by allowing savers and investors more opportunity to diversify their assets and liabilities. Such benefits are analogous to the gains from international trade that widen world consumption possibilities.

TRADE-RELATED INVESTMENT BENEFITS

The trend toward increasing foreign investment in the United States is part of a larger trend toward globalization and international economic interdependence. This increased integration can already be seen in the international trade in goods and services. And as with the globalization in trade, the globalization in investment results in increased efficiency.

International trade boosts efficiency in three ways. First, trade allows each country to concentrate on producing those goods and services in which it has a comparative advantage. Second, trade increases competition and thereby gives companies continuing incentives for efficiency, innovation, and excellence. Third, it impels countries to adapt more quickly and efficiently to the changing world economy. The costs associated with such adjustment are sometimes serious, but they are generally outweighed by the benefits. As a result, overall economic growth and prosperity are enhanced.

Well-placed foreign investment can help a country to augment its advantages from trade. It can finance the building and equipping of larger and/or more productive facilities, thus enabling a country to market still more of the goods and services it produces best. These goods and services can then be added to the country's exports or substituted for its imports, resulting in foreign exchange earnings or savings that are greater than the cost of servicing the foreign investment. Foreign investment can also finance the entry of new firms into the marketplace, thereby adding to competitive pressures. Through the establishment of new firms, foreign investment can also create new jobs. It can finance the purchase of new equipment to incorporate the latest technology, thus enabling the country to adjust more quickly to changing world competitive conditions.

Certain economic benefits from foreign investment are most quickly and efficiently transferred to another country through *direct* investment channels (i.e., through a firm's foreign subsidiaries or an appropriately designed joint venture). Newly discovered technological advances are a good example. Because information markets are imperfect and research and development (R & D) knowledge is often hard to patent, a company may be wary of sharing its new technology with independent firms for fear that it may be copied by a rival that spent no such money on R & D. One possible solution is to enter into licensing arrangements with foreign firms that ensure some protection and profit, but sometimes even these arrangements do not satisfy a company with a keenly proprietary feeling about its product technology. On the other hand, if the same firm has directly invested in foreign subsidiaries, it can produce and distribute the good or service through those subsidiaries without significant fear that the competitive advantage of a new technological discovery will be quickly lost.

These benefits of direct investment are strong enough that foreign direct investments in the United States, and also direct investments abroad by U.S. firms, are likely to continue to grow in gross total over the decades, irrespective of what happens to the net balance

BROADER SOCIOECONOMIC BENEFITS

Foreign *direct* investment also provides broader socioeconomic benefits for the United States. It brings valuable resources into our economy including technology, know-how, management, training, and facilities for marketing products or services. It can stimulate production in other sectors where a scarcity of inputs may be relieved by the products of the foreign-owned enterprise. It encourages domestic entrepreneurship by purchasing from or subcontracting to local suppliers, trains workers in new skills and indirectly spreads this knowledge to other labor force participants.

Sometimes U.S. subsidiaries of foreign firms are criticized for staying "too foreign" in their purchase of component parts and in their selection of managers. Most often, however, any inclinations in this direction tend to wane over time as the subsidiary becomes more familiar with U.S. sources of supply and managerial talent, and as U.S. suppliers adapt their product to the specifications of the foreign-owned subsidiary. Such adaptations, in due course, typically seem to improve the general performance of the U.S. suppliers.

All told, foreign direct investment adds to the U.S. economy's real output and income by an amount greater than what accrues to the direct investor. As a result, many sectors of the economy benefit: labor in the form of more employment and higher wages, consumers in the form of lower prices and a wider choice of better-quality products, and government in the form of larger tax revenues.

Moreover, the direct participation in American business of internationally-oriented foreign companies may improve U.S. export performance by opening up new marketing opportunities abroad for products manufactured in the United States.

In sum, the external effects of foreign direct investment, although not conventional, are nonetheless beneficial. Admittedly, these kinds of effects are difficult to measure quantitatively, but it is important to bear in mind that they do exist and are a potentially significant part of our economy.

6. What Are the Biggest Potential Drawbacks of Such Heavy Net Foreign Investment Flows into the United States?

In discussing the startling increase in foreign investment in the United States, more emphasis ought to be placed on the *type* of foreign investment that has been taking place. The chief focus of recent public attention has been on the growing rate of foreign *direct* investment. Increasing foreign portfolio investment has been largely ignored; yet, it is *portfolio* investment that warrants the most concern.

Fears are sometimes expressed that foreign owners of controlling interests in U.S. firms will use their control to "dumb down" their U.S. subsidiaries, keeping their technologically advanced R & D in or near their own headquarters. Although individual efforts of this type could be launched by foreign firms, as they can be by domestic firms, the available evidence does not show this as a typical outcome. In fact, a recent study by Graham and Krugman indicates that U.S. manufacturing subsidiaries of foreign firms on average operate with a slightly higher rate of R & D expenditures than U.S.-owned manufacturing firms do. Nor do the authors find any tendency for foreign-owned manufacturing facilities in the United States to employ lower-paid workers than their U.S.-owned counterparts. When it comes to monopolistic practices in this country, foreign-owned firms are subject to the same set of legal prohibitions and penalties as U.S.-owned firms (see answer to question 8 for details). There is need, however, for U.S. authorities enforcing these laws to take updated account of foreign-based as well as domestic-based competition in judging what constitutes excessive concentration of market power.

Direct investment, in the form of real estate or plant purchases, implies a long-term commitment to the U.S. economy. Often, a significant share of the earnings of these foreign-owned direct investments is reinvested in this country. In addition, the markets for direct investment are more self-disciplined than the financial markets for portfolio investment. The risk of foreign investors dumping their direct investment holdings is therefore significantly less, simply because these assets are not as liquid. Even during periods of financial crisis, these investments cannot simply be sold overnight.

In contrast, *portfolio* investment consists mostly of liquid financial assets that, by their very nature, *can* be sold overnight. In times of unstable financial markets (the most recent being the Black Monday episode of October 1987), anxious foreign investors can try to quickly sell a disproportionate part of their portfolio holdings. The resulting attempt at sudden and large liquidation of foreign-held securities can have highly adverse effects on the U.S. economy by sharply weakening the dollar and pushing up interest rates. The risk of financial instability is therefore a real drawback, even though we cannot predict exactly whether, when, and how much financial instability will actually erupt.

Debt burden is a second important drawback and a more certain one. Whereas foreign direct investment in the United States does not typically represent a debt held beyond our national borders that we must service and later repay, indirect investment in the form of securities and bank deposits typically does. Both gross and net foreign-held U.S. debts in these forms are rapidly rising, as is the associated growing foreign debt-service burden (see Figure 8). It has already caught up with the expanding total of income earned by Americans on their investments in foreign countries, and it is surging ahead at an even faster clip.

When U.S. debt burgeons, servicing that debt (i.e., paying interest, dividends, and related charges on the securities owned by others) becomes more burdensome whether the debt is held by fellow Americans or foreigners. However, paying debt service to foreign debt holders involves the extra disadvantages of putting those funds in the hands of holders less likely to spend them in the United States and more likely to use them in ways that put downward pressure on the foreign exchange rate of the dollar.

Each of these influences works to cut into Americans' future standard of living.

A third drawback is that the proceeds of much of recent foreign *portfolio* investment in American securities and bank deposits had seemed to end up financing more American consumption. This is a direct result of our national economic policies and attitudes. If, instead, we began to behave responsibly by curtailing government and private consumption, foreign capital inflow could be used to finance more productive investment. For example, it could increase American output of quality goods and services (especially exportable goods and services). It could thereby help us develop more wherewithal to service our future foreign debt burden and in the long run decrease our international current-account deficits.

A noteworthy example of this productive capacity of foreign portfolio investment is the period in the nineteenth century when British capital was invested to help build railroads in the United States. As a result of this investment, jobs were created, efficiency of transport increased, and transportation costs decreased.

We do not see enough of this type of utilization of the proceeds of foreign portfolio investment in the United States. Our debt-service burden is therefore all the more worrisome because the great bulk of portfolio investment inflow does not seem to be invested in ways that will help us to develop more wherewithal to service our foreign debt in the future.

---

7. Are Foreign-Owned Plants a Threat to U.S. National Security?

As foreign investors buy into U.S. manufacturing firms making products or conducting research important to American military strength, it is not surprising that concerns arise about the effects on our national security. That question can even arise when foreign firms build "greenfield" plants (i.e., completely new plants) here to compete with such U.S. firms.

An objective look at those possibilities, however, indicates that the practical risks are small and that the U.S. government has the wherewithal to guard against them.

First, the foreign owners of those plants have business reasons for not operating in ways that threaten U.S. national security. They need to be viewed favorably by both their U.S. customers and the U.S. government in order to continue to operate profitably in this country. Any action by the foreign-owned firm prejudicial to U.S. security would risk reversal of those favorable views and swift retaliatory action.

Nonetheless, as safeguards, various preventive measures are provided for by our government. Like other developed countries, the United States has imposed restrictions on foreign direct investment in certain sectors for national security reasons. Various statutes incorporate these restrictions, including the Atomic Energy Act, the Federal Aviation Act, the Shipping Act, and the Federal Communications Act. The latest addition to such U.S. government powers is the Exon-Florio Amendment, which is summed up as follows in the 1990 *Economic Report of the President:*

> Under the Exon-Florio provision of the Omnibus Trade and Competitiveness Act of 1988, the interagency Committee on Foreign Investment in the United States reviews investments with potential national security implications and investigates sensitive transactions. The President can prohibit or suspend investments that threaten to impair U.S. national security. By the end of 1989, this committee had reviewed more than 200 transactions, undertaken investigations of 6 and referred 3 to the President for a decision. In each case, the President decided not to intervene. In line with the Administration's open investment policy and the provision of law, the Exon-Florio authority will be used only when no other measures are adequate to protect the national security.[2]

Among the other measures that could be used, the Defense Department's contracting power is a strong one. If a foreign-owned firm in the United States is making a product needed for U.S. military purposes, the department can negotiate a procurement contract with the firm that contains various safeguards. These could include special plant inspection and surveillance, restricted access to any sensitive U.S. technology involved, assured minimum production capacity for the product in their U.S. plants, assured minimum share of product R & D done in facilities in the United States, and/or even quotas for the number of U.S. citizens to be employed in sensitive positions. In sum, these options give the U.S. government a powerful arsenal of measures to utilize in cases where national security is deemed to be at risk in purchasing from a foreign-owned firm.

One way of protecting the national security interest, of course, is to make sensitive defense purchases from domestic plants of U.S. firms capable of turning out a world-class product without any U.S. government sheltering from fair foreign competition, if such firms can be found. Staying globally competitive will impel such firms to be in the forefront in technological advances, quality control, and productive efficiency, thus keeping the U.S. industrial base for that product strong. The U.S. government, for its part, needs to be careful not to handicap the capabilities of such firms to measure up to these challenging competitive standards.*

---

[2]*Economic Report of the President* (Washington, D.C.: U.S. Government Printing Office, 1990).

*See memorandum by JAMES J. RENIER, (Page 32.)

8. How Can We Be Sure Foreign-Owned Companies in the United States Will Behave Responsibly?

The best way to develop a responsible answer to this question is to look at how we ensure that U.S.-owned firms behave responsibly. Two major mechanisms for promoting proper business behavior are relied upon: the discipline imposed by *market forces* and that imposed by *U.S. government laws and regulations*. Both are being used, or can be used, to ensure that a foreign-owned firm in our country behaves as responsibly as a U.S.-owned firm. However, these mechanisms need to be used effectively in order to achieve that goal, and in some cases that will require more alert and vigorous actions than are now typical.

Perhaps the most pervasive and often underrated market discipline on foreign firms that undertake operations in the United States is information— knowledge and appreciation of the behavioral norms for companies in this country. U.S.-owned firms and their American managers and employees receive such information in countless natural ways as they grow up in our culture. There is no master manual easily available that foreign firms can read to learn how to behave here.

However, this is a gap that does not have to persist. For example, national, state, and local Chambers of Commerce can develop one or an assortment of manuals on behavioral norms in U.S. business and provide them to managements of foreign-owned firms. States and localities have economic development agencies that actively recruit foreign firms to locate in their areas; they could provide such firms with pamphlets outlining the business behavior norms expected in their areas. This flow of helpful information need not be a one-way street. Because a foreign-owned company's behavior is different in some respects does not necessarily mean it is wrong. For example, the concept of a worker team responsible for keeping quality high on the production line, popularized by certain Japanese firms, was thought questionable for American workers until some Japanese transplants in this country demonstrated its effectiveness. Now many American-owned plants are making very effective use of that quality-control technique to help them regain world-class competitiveness.

A more difficult problem is posed if a foreign-owned firm learns American norms and still wishes to persist in some policy or practice that U.S. society regards as wrong. In such cases, there is a family of corrective pressures that U.S. market forces can bring to bear. The most practical is U.S. *customer pressure* if the firm's customers are adversely affected by the offensive action. Shrinking sales in the U.S. market send a powerful message to a foreign management.

In addition, many civic, labor, and other groups in America have proved ingenious in developing ways to express their objections to behavior by U.S. firms that they regard as undesirable. Oftentimes, such efforts are enhanced by pressure from a *civic and media* coalition when the newspapers or other media outlets are convinced of the justice of the complaints. These efforts also can and undoubtedly will be brought to bear increasingly on foreign-owned firms here as the foreign presence in the United States keeps growing.

Powerful though these market forces may be, there are still circumstances in which the force of *government laws and regulations* is needed to achieve enough comprehensive, timely, and enduring deterrence of damagingly irresponsible behavior by foreign-owned firms. The United States has a great many laws and regulations to protect consumers and the general public that are applicable to both foreign-owned and U.S.-owned companies producing and selling products and services in the American market. These measures are in accordance with the broadly accepted standard of "national treatment" and are enforced by financial penalties if violated.

In general, to minimize jurisdictional problems between home and host countries, where conflicts exist host-country law should take precedence. That means U.S. law should govern in conflicts involving foreign investments in the United States. However, because not all disputes can be resolved by any simple rule, bilateral or multilateral agreements between the home country and the United States are needed regarding the treatment of foreign investment in order to establish more specific jurisdictional principles and/or provide mutually acceptable procedures for the settlement of conflicts.

9. Is Foreign Ownership of U.S. Real Estate Bad?

It may wound our pride when we see noteworthy real estate such as the Waikiki Beach oceanfront and Rockefeller Center purchased by foreign owners. But those and similar foreign purchases of real estate add up to only a small fraction of the total of U.S. property, and they are not bad when compared realistically with the alternatives we face at this stage. The level and growth of foreign ownership of U.S. real estate between 1980 and 1989 are shown in Figure 9, page 26, measured in terms of *book* value.

The truth is that Americans have been buying so much more in the way of tradable products from abroad than they are selling abroad at current prices and exchange rates that there has to be a big reverse flow back into the United States in the form of foreign-owned dollars to be invested. (The answers to questions 2 and 4 point that out.) Until this country straightens out the macroeconomic and trade policy mismatches and shortfalls in export industry perfor-

FIGURE 9

Foreign Real Estate Holdings in the United States, 1980 to 1989

Billions of Dollars in Book Value

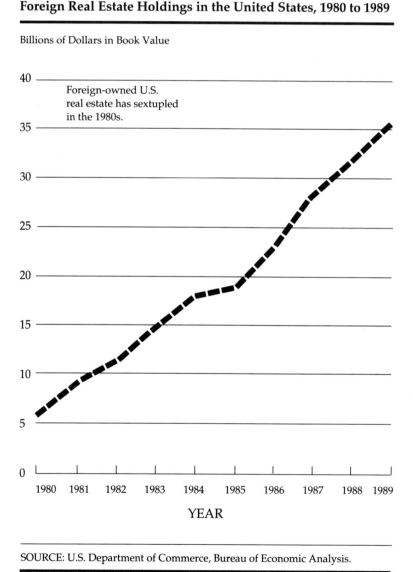

YEAR

SOURCE: U.S. Department of Commerce, Bureau of Economic Analysis.

mance that give rise to such big net flows across national borders, large-scale foreign investment inflow will continue.[3]

That means our present policies are, in effect, entitling foreigners to buy U.S. capital assets at a fast pace. The most convenient assets for them to buy are portfolio assets (i.e., U.S. government securities, marketable bonds and stocks, money market securities, and certificates of deposit). However, if these build up to uncomfortably large totals for their foreign holders, they may become a source of trouble. What is quickly and easily bought can also be quickly and easily sold. As we indicated in the answer to question 6, an excessively large buildup of U.S. portfolio assets in foreign hands can pose a serious risk of financial instability.

The other major types of U.S. capital assets foreigners buy are real estate and controlling shares in business ventures. These direct investments—about one-tenth of which are in real estate—have accounted for almost one-third of total foreign acquisitions of U.S. capital assets throughout the 1980s (see questions 1 and 2). The cumulative total of such real estate acquisitions still amounts to less than 5 percent of total U.S. real estate.

Such direct investments, by their nature, are not so quickly sold. They tend to be held for the longer term, and their foreign owners therefore have more reason to be interested in the national, regional, and community factors that enhance our capital values over time. In addition, the foreign owners of such direct investments may provide other valuable inputs besides money to their ventures (see question 5).

It should be noted, however, that large swings in the dollar's foreign exchange rates, such as result from major mismatches between U.S. and foreign fiscal and monetary policies, can markedly alter the buying power of foreigners interested in investing in U.S. plants and real estate. If that sharply changed buying power is focused on some narrow U.S. markets, it can have disproportionate effects upon them.

10. Do the Pluses of Foreign Investment in the United States Add Up to More than the Minuses?

The right answer to this question is a resounding yes. The foundations of these net gains are chiefly the three special forces that enable trade between reasonably open economies to benefit both parties (see question 5).

[3]CED urges that such policy changes be made promptly. For details on what needs to be done, see CED's publications *Battling America's Budget Deficits, Investing in America's Future,* and *Breaking New Ground in U.S. Trade Policy.*

Trade-related foreign investment can enhance those trading advantages that the country can realize with its own resources (again, see question 5). The more that foreign capital inflow focuses on productive investment opportunities in the United States, the greater the net benefit that is likely to ensue. Probably the most beneficial to the United States at this time is foreign direct investment that funds the production of exportable products or import substitutes, the foreign exchange earnings or savings of which are greater than the cost of servicing the foreign investment. However, even foreign investment in U.S. government securities can help importantly by lowering capital costs and leaving more domestic investable funds free to seek such productive opportunities.

There are, of course, minuses to foreign investment in the United States that need to be weighed against these benefits. Some of those minuses are problematic or otherwise hard to quantify, but they are nonetheless real and deserve to be judged in the balance. The biggest drawbacks (see question 6) flow from the fast-rising foreign-held U.S. debt and its consequences. Because so small a portion of the proceeds of that debt is being utilized by Americans to finance productive activities that earn (or save) foreign exchange, we can look forward to a steadily rising net foreign debt-service burden that will, in effect, subtract from the living standard of future generations of Americans. Moreover, that burgeoning debt total, preponderantly in forms easily sold or cashed, should be recognized for the potential threat of financial instability it poses.

However, that threat can probably be moderated somewhat by appropriate corrections in U.S. government policies and improved U.S. industrial competitiveness, even if the concrete results of those actions take some years to manifest themselves. Such U.S. policy changes should in due course moderate the big imbalances in U.S. trade and investment flows, thereby rendering the structure of international trade and investment more stable and sustainable even as the forces of globalization encourage continuing growth in the gross volumes of cross-border flows.

Weighing all these factors, we believe the evidence conclusively supports the judgment that well-placed foreign trade and investment yield impressive net benefits over time that can be shared by all participants: workers, businesses, consumers, investors, and governments in the United States as the host country and in the country from which the investment comes. The relative sizes of those shares can vary, depending on the circumstances, and often there can be quite a squabble over changing share sizes. Such squabbles, however, should not be allowed to overshadow the basic truth that, over time, there can be more for all.

11. Do We Need More International Rules Regarding Foreign Direct Investment?

The time is ripe for a major initiative to develop uniform international standards for foreign direct investment in all countries. A strong multilateral investment agreement would make the mutual gains from foreign investment larger for all participants. In order for these gains to be realized, each participant should understand the other's goals and interests and adjust its own policies in a spirit of mutual accommodation. The best way to accomplish this on a fair and uniform basis would be to establish a comprehensive international agreement along the lines of GATT that would cover investment across national borders.

The main obstacle to such an agreement earlier in the post-World War II era was the threat U.S. economic dominance was thought to pose to the sovereignty of smaller nations. Today, however, the United States has become the major host country to foreign direct investment, and Western Europe has superseded it as the source of more than half of such flows. At the same time, Japan has become the approximate equal of the United States as a source of foreign direct investment flows to industrializing countries. This more balanced distribution of foreign investment reduces the fears of U.S. dominance and creates a basis for common concerns and shared policy interests. The political climate in developing countries is also more favorable to foreign investment than in the past.

A GATT-style international agreement covering investment across national borders would also benefit U.S. investors abroad, who frequently face restrictions on access to local distribution facilities (including transportation and communications networks), limitations on rights of establishment, discriminatory taxes or regulations, and other deviations from national treatment. Given the overall openness of the United States to foreign investment, U.S. firms understandably believe they deserve comparable treatment when investing abroad. An international code of conduct could help future U.S. investment abroad and therefore help this country to reinforce its world-leadership role.

For these reasons, the United States should prepare immediately to pursue a comprehensive international agreement covering investment across national borders following the scheduled conclusion of the Uruguay Round of GATT negotiations at the end of 1990. The most practical arena in which to press such negotiations is the Organization for Economic Cooperation and Development (OECD) with the other developed countries that are its members, but these negotiations should be open to participation by non-OECD countries that share their objectives. The new accord should address national treatment; rights of establishment (subject to exceptions for reasons of national security and public order); expropriation, compensation, and free transfer of funds (not problems among OECD nations, but important for industrializing countries that may wish to sign); dispute settlement (which might include use of the International Chamber of Commerce's Arbitration Court or the World Bank's International Center for the Settlement of Investment Disputes); and special incentives and disincentives. The issue of trade-related investment measures (TRIMs), such as export targeting and local-content requirements, should be left within the purview of GATT, which already includes a legal basis for preventing such practices. TRIMs negotiations are proceeding under GATT auspices, and the broader OECD negotiations recommended here should be conducted in complementary fashion.

The proposed OECD investment agreement should be left open to later accession by non-OECD nations, including developing countries, newly industrialized countries (NICs), and the economies of Eastern Europe as they develop freer commercial dealings with the West. But for the present, the majority of developing countries and NICs are probably not quite ready to sign such a far-reaching accord.

In such cases, the United States should continue to seek to establish better standards for foreign investment by negotiating individual bilateral treaties with each developing nation. Worldwide, almost 300 such bilateral treaties have already been signed. Since the U.S. bilateral investment treaty program was begun in 1981, agreements have been reached with ten countries: Egypt, Morocco, Turkey, Senegal, Zaire, Grenada, Bangladesh, Cameroon, Panama, and Haiti. (The Panama and Haiti agreements were later withdrawn by the Administration for political reasons.)

When negotiating similar treaties in the future, the U.S. government should be both patient and flexible. For example, more limited agreements could be reached initially with developing countries that are hesitant to accept drastic changes to their current investment practices. The United States could then stipulate that such treaties be limited to a specifically defined period. Such treaties would provide a stepping-stone toward a full bilateral agreement.

The treaties with developing countries should place particular emphasis on provisions for dispute settlement, transfer of funds, and expropriation and compensation. Other standards, such as rights of establishment (which would necessitate a long list of exceptions) and performance requirements, could be agreed upon in later treaties. If necessary to reach accord, the United States should also be willing to agree that national treatment and most-favored-nation principles apply only to future investment. Such concessions would accelerate the number and pace of negotiations with those developing countries that are the most promising locations for future U.S. foreign investment.

* * *

We hope these questions and answers have helped to clarify the role that foreign investment is playing in U.S. economic developments and what its implications are. If you would like more detailed information on these issues, we refer you to the list of lengthier publications by CED and others on page 33.

Memoranda of Comment, Reservation, or Dissent

Page 17, JAMES Q. RIORDAN, with which EDMUND B. FITZGERALD has asked to be associated.

I approve the statement for publication. It makes the case for liberal and fair global investment rules. It also points out the need for the U.S. to increase its savings and reduce its current consumption in order to be better able to participate in the global investment process and to assure an improving U.S. standard of living in the future. The statement would have been improved had we restated the tax policy positions taken in earlier statements — namely, we need to revise our tax structure to reduce existing biases against savings and investment (and in favor of consumption) and to eliminate biases against U.S. business seeking to make profitable foreign investments.

Page 23, JAMES J. RENIER

Generally, I think it is a good, well-balanced paper that puts many of the issues in the proper perspective.

My most serious reservation about the paper pertains to the treatment it gives to the national security issue. I believe the paper understates the potential significance of the issue.

CED Reference Statements

Breaking New Ground in United States Trade Policy (1990).

Finance and Third World Economic Growth (1988).

New Dynamics in the Global Economy (1988).

Strengthening U.S.-Japan Economic Relations (1989).

Toll of the Twin Deficits (1987).

Transnational Corporations and Developing Countries (1981).

Who Should Be Liable? A Guide to Policy for Dealing with Risk (1989).

Other Reference Documents

Graham, Edward H., and Paul R. Krugman. *Foreign Direct Investment in the United States.* Washington, D.C.: Institute for International Economics, 1989.

Stekler, Lois, and Guy Stevens, "The Adequacy of U.S. Direct Investment Data." In P. Hooper and J. Richardson (eds.), *International Economic Transactions: Issues in Measurement and Empirical Research.* Chicago: Chicago University Press. Forthcoming.

U.S. Department of Commerce, Bureau of Economic Analysis. *Survey of Current Business.* Washington, D.C.: U.S. Government Printing Office, various issues.

Economic Report of the President. Washington, D.C.: U.S. Government Printing Office, 1990.

Note: Copies of the above-cited CED publications can be obtained by calling or writing:

Committee for Economic Development

477 Madison Avenue, 6th Floor, New York, NY 10022   (212) 688-2063

1700 K Street, N.W., Suite 700, Washington, D.C. 20006   (202) 296-5860

Objectives of the Committee for Economic Development

For over forty years, the Committee for Economic Development has been a respected influence on the formation of business and public policy. CED is devoted to these two objectives:

To develop, through objective research and informed discussion, findings and recommendations for private and public policy that will contribute to preserving and strengthening our free society, achieving steady economic growth at high employment and reasonably stable prices, increasing productivity and living standards, providing greater and more equal opportunity for every citizen, and improving the quality of life for all.

To bring about increasing understanding by present and future leaders in business, government, and education, and among concerned citizens, of the importance of these objectives and the ways in which they can be achieved.

CED's work is supported by private voluntary contributions from business and industry, foundations, and individuals. It is independent, non-profit, nonpartisan, and non-political.

Through this business-academic partnership, CED endeavors to develop policy statements and other research materials that commend themselves as guides to public and business policy; that can be used as texts in college economics and political science courses and in management training courses; that will be considered and discussed by newspaper and magazine editors, columnists, and commentators; and that are distributed abroad to promote better understanding of the American economic system.

CED believes that by enabling business leaders to demonstrate constructively their concern for the general welfare, it is helping business to earn and maintain the national and community respect essential to the successful functioning of the free enterprise capitalist system.

CED BOARD OF TRUSTEES

CED HONORARY TRUSTEES

75815
43

Committee for Economic Development
477 Madison Avenue
New York, New York 10022